THE NAME IT
and
CLAIM IT GAME

with

WINeuvers for WISHcraft

by

HELEN HADSELL

DeVorss & Co., *Publishers*
P.O. Box 550
Marina Del Rey, Ca. 90291

Delta Sciences
P.O. Box 456
Cleburne, TX 76031

Fourth Printing, 1978

ISBN 0-87516-119-7

Library of Congress Catalogue Number: 70-184915

Order autographed books from
Helen Hadsell, address above.
$2.50 plus 25 cents postage per package.

Printed in the United States of America
by Book Graphics, Inc., Marina del Rey, California

CONTENTS

Introduction 5

The Name It and Claim It Game 7

Let Dike Win This One . . . He Is More Patriotic Than I 16

All Things Come to HIM Who Waits 21

Yes . . . You Can 33

Now Act Surprised . . . They Expect It 39

How To Be Successful Without Really Trying 46

Hunches Are The Handiest Things 52

The Supreme Test 59

What's Taking You So Long? 67

WINeuvers For WISHcraft 77

3

INTRODUCTION

An Exciting Challenge for You The Reader: Learn How You Can Play the Game of Life to Win with Positive Thinking.

You may find this a bold and egotistical book. I hope you do. You may also find ideas that can guide you in transforming your life. It can change you from a loser to a winner . . . that is if you want to change.

Why was this book written? It was written for men and women who are unhappy and dissatisfied with their present status. Most of all, it is for you who are willing to challenge your present ideas about life and change them when necessary.

What is the key to success—the key that opens the Magic Box where all the goodies of life are stored? It is the mind, the vast computer that has the secrets of the universe and life itself. So much awaits us when we become aware of mind and are in control.

We can finally learn why things happen to us, what places us in control of our fortunes.

No person and no circumstance can disturb our inner peace. Fear and tension vanish when you use positive control. Heartache and headache are exposed and dissolved. Everything becomes right when we learn to love and live this new way.

You, the reader, possess all the capacities for self-enrichment. You need only to exercise these powers. As you begin, have no concern whether you are proceeding correctly. Just begin.

Helen Hadsell

CHAPTER I

The Name It and Claim It Game

The truly successful person is the positive thinking one.

The more you cultivate and control a positive attitude, the more successful you become. As you develop positive thinking, success replaces failure until you no longer can fail.

No matter your past or present — you can change the future. Everyone has a different idea of what success is. To some, being successful in their love pursuits is the ultimate goal. Some seek health and body building programs, while others want fame and fortune. And then there are those who need huge homes, cars and money as a determining factor.

Unfortunately some don't know what they want. They scatter their desires into so many avenues that they never really accumulate enough energy to make anything manifest for them. They run hot and cold, up and down, in and out of projects, never really stopping long enough to analyze why they are not successful. They never fully accept the idea that with a positive attitude and control they can actually materialize anything they need or want on the physical plane.

The following personal experiences which I share with you are not to tell you how great I am

. . . but to clue you in on just how great you are. And is there not a saying that tells you so? — "All these things that I do...you can do, and more."

Twelve years ago, 1959 to be exact, my idea of success was to be able to enter contests and win . . . win . . . win anything and everything that one could possess in this material world. I developed a desire, a goal, and a determination. I had read a book on positive thinking, and it left an indelible impression. So I was out to prove to myself that anything the mind can conceive and believe, it can achieve with positive thinking.

STEP NUMBER 1. Set a goal. If you *know* what you *want* you can *have* it. I must make one thing clear in regard to entering contests since there are sometimes misconceptions as to wins — why, and how one wins. I had no background, such as a writing talent, nor had I taken any writing courses at that time. I did not know any people who work for judging firms. In other words I had no "pull".

My first experiment began when my husband expressed a desire to own an outboard motor since he enjoyed fishing. He called my attention to a contest sponsored by a soft drink firm. The prizes were outboard motors. The requirement was to complete a sentence in 25 words or less on why you liked to take Coke on your outings.

My one entry was this: "I take Cokes on outings because I'm a lone-wolf fisherman and Coke is my silent partner. It contributes no yakaty-yak, only cool, refreshing enjoyment when called upon".

I came upon this idea when I imagined I was my

8

husband, so I naturally wrote from his viewpoint. He certainly did like to go fishing by his lonesome— that is until the two boys were old enough to enjoy fishing trips with him.

Three weeks after the contest closed, the phone rang and a company representative informed us that we had indeed won an outboard motor.

I confess that prior to the announcement that we had won, every time the thought crossed my mind about the contest or the motor, I "convinced" myself again I would win. I was so determined to be positive I even asked myself, 'I wonder when they will let us know that we have won?' I had no negative doubts, such as, 'I'll bet the contest is rigged.' (I'd heard that one quite often). Nor did I entertain the thought that I wasn't lucky. I also heard that only clever people win. (Now how does one acquire cleverness? Why, one works at it). So you see, I refused to entertain any negative doubts.

STEP NUMBER 2. Never entertain doubts. this nullifies all good strong, powerful positive currents.

The second contest I entered was a jingle type where one had to complete a last line. The prize was a second telephone installed in your home with the bills paid for a year. I thought how convenient it would be if I could have a phone installed in the kitchen, since I spent most of my time in that part of the house.

When I sent off my three entries, I used the same positive thinking I had applied to my "motor win". I knew I would be a winner, and again I questioned how long it would take the company to inform me.

It took five weeks after the contest closed before I received the letter telling me I was a winner. I had no way of knowing which entry actually won.

In the meantime we decided to move into a larger home and moved from Grand Prairie to Irving, Texas. The company that sponsored the telephone contest was kind enough to send a check in lieu of the phone service for a year rather than transfer the paper work to another exchange.

By now the family was quite impressed with mother, who had made two attempts at entering contests and won both. In the next few efforts to win contests, the family joined in.

Next a request came from my daughter, Pamela, then 16 years old. She wanted a bicycle. She called my attention to a contest advertisement in the Sunday paper comic section. We got so carried away this time that we submitted seven entries. The requirements were to name a pony. She won a girl's blue bicycle four weeks after the contest closed. We had no way of determining which one of the names actually impressed the judges, but we did have great fun in being creative and coining original apt names. Following are the names that we sent: FootPrince, HimBUCKtoo, Fancy Prance, Stirup Dust, StanPedro, Twinkle Toes, and Prance Charmin'.

Our ten year old son, Dike, was next to put in his bid. He, too, wanted a shiny new bicycle. At that time a candy contest was in progress, and top prizes were bicycles. We were to complete in 15 words why we liked their candy product. Again, we made a family project of writing ideas, and in this endeavor we submitted four entries. Now the children were so sure we just had to win, that we all waited for the mailman to bring us the letter making it official. We now realized that it took from two to six weeks after a contest closed before the winners would be notified. But, of course he won the bicycle. This time we were interested in which entry actually would win the prize so we came up with this method. We submitted the first entry in my son's full name Dike O'Kane Hadsell. The second entry we used only Dike Hadsell. The third signature was Dike O. Hadsell and the fourth was signed D. O. Hadsell. This way we were able to determine the winning fifteen words were: "So colorful, so neat, so nice and plump, they're nutritious pick-ups for mid-day slump". (The letter was addressed to the name that we used to submit this entry). We were describing why we liked candy coated licorice pieces.

This idea of keying entries was not original with us, as later we learned that quite a few contestants used this method to key their entries and learn which one of their brain children actually wins the prize.

About this time, there were so many contests with so many prizes, one had a choice of what one wanted, which to enter, etc. or, perhaps we had only become more aware of opportunities for obtaining the things one would like to have in life.

I might inject this for anyone who sees this as luck — the fact that we did win the first time we entered, helped us gain confidence. There is a cliche that goes like this, 'If at first you don't succeed try, try, again!' Had I not won my first try, I feel certain the positive attitude would have urged me to continue to enter regardless.

I have since realized that with a positive thinking outlook there is no failure—only a delay in results. *Something to think about.* The imaging faculty played a leading part in the goals I wished to achieve. So I recommend, to play successfully we train the imaging faculty. A person who trains himself to success, brings success into his life.

As I mentioned earlier when I became aware of contesting, I realized just how many were going on nation-wide, including local ones. There are currently approximately 150 contests available for the average person to enter. I learned that an excellent source for creative writing and contesting information material is: Shepherd School, P.O. Box 333, Willingboro, NJ 08046. Enclose 75¢ for a sample copy of their material. A good source for sweepstakes information is: National Sweepstakes and Contest Guide, P.O. Box 2688, West Palm Beach, Fla. 33402. Enclose 60¢ for a sample copy of their material.

If you wish to pursue the hobby you might like to see one of the issues. With all this information on hand it was like a Wish Book. If any item appealed to us, that was the contest we worked on to win. Suffice it to say, we won bats, balls, radios, dolls, games, electrical appliances, cash prizes . . . in other words you name it and I'll claim it. I was reluctant (at that time) to vie for any contests that offered trips because I was afraid to fly. I had already told myself that if I did win a trip I would not take it, so I never gave that type any consideration or energy. In other words I was content with comforts like blankets, bicycles and basics. But that soon changed.

One day my younger son Chris, age 8, saw a contest of a trip for youngsters to a Dude Ranch in Arizona. He thought that it might be family fun. I wanted to go but flying was out of the question. However, we did enter the contest. To make a long story short, we won the trip. Again, this contest called for children to name a pony. We submitted the same names we used in the other pony naming contest, and noted that the name StamPedro was the winner. When the forms came about the schedules, etc. I requested we be allowed to go by train. I refused to go by plane. I did not realize it was a pre-packaged deal for the winners, and fly you must. When I refused we were disqualified. We did, however, receive a second prize of a movie camera. But my son was very disappointed. When I had time to consider the immaturity of my groundless fear of air travel, I had to do some powerful positive thinking to convince myself planes are quite safe. I told myself I would enjoy flying and in the future I would enter contests and vie for trips because they would be fun. In other words I was connin' myself for the big lift.

I finally convinced myself with all that tall positive thinking that the only way to go is to fly. I called this *The Die As You Fly* program because I was scared stiff.

STEP NUMBER 3. You can con yourself into anything by repeating it over and over again until you incorporate it into your thinking—that is the way it is. Sometimes it takes longer but I have found it is a very effective sure-fire method once you incorporate it into your conscious thinking program.

A family dude ranch trip again was offered the following summer in a children's contest and this time I informed the family this would be our summer vacation. This particular contest was sponsored by a Ranch Style Bean company and it merely required one to submit his name on the back of a label. It was a sweepstake type contest. Of course we won it, and of course we flew. To say I did not have apprehension would be a big fat lie as I recall all during the trip I was (in-fright) trance and convincing myself how great it was. (Who was I to tell the family that if God had wanted us to fly he would have given us wings). The family had such a great time that I could not deprive them of future fun trips they were now anticipating. I also did further reprogramming and told myself next trip I'd open my eyes and eat meals served on the plane. I was told the food was quite delicious.

The next year we won a first prize of a family trip to Disneyland. My younger son, Chris, "the fly-hi boy" that insisted we win trips, was bugged by the family to draw the ugliest bug he could conjure up for this big win. Talk about excitement, that really was one of the hi-lights in the Hadsell family's fun and game times. The trip was so delightful I could have kissed the judges and sponsors (imagine kissing perfect strangers, because I still had never met one).

14

May I say in our experience of contest winning the prizes were always more than we had anticipated. If we won an appliance it was always the latest model, the representatives from the companies were most kind and usually we got things not included on the prize list. Our trip to Disneyland stipulated a trip for a family of four. There are five Hadsells. Yet they included all of us, gave us extra passbooks for the park activities at Disneyland plus a generous spending allowance. It was beautiful.

CHAPTER II

Let Dike Win This One . . .
He is More Patriotic Than I

After the five day family holiday on the Dude Ranch and the Disneyland trip, the boys' appetites were whetted for more travel and trip wins.

The next opportunity for a trip that presented itself and proved interesting was geared for high school students. Requirements were to complete a 250 word essay on "My Responsibility to America". Two winners from each state would win a trip to the nation's capital for three days of touring and listening to government officials. The contest was sponsored by the Rexall Drug stores. I had noticed the blanks in the store one day and brought one home.

That evening at the dinner table I was explaining the contest to the boys and elaborating on what an advantage it would be to visit Washington, D.C. I asked which one might like to make the trip. They both thought it over momentarily, then Chris said, "Let Dike have this one, he is more patriotic than I".

"OK, deadline is eight days from now so better do some serious thinking and get it on paper," I suggested.

May I say that after several years of contesting, I was still the one that stimulated the interest it took to get rolling on a new one. The family pool of offering encouragement, suggestions and ideas plus their positive thinking made it a most gratifying family fun and game activity.

Dike's entry was so sincere and warm that when I read it I could find only one mistake and that was in spelling. In my estimation, it was a sure winner. Now all that was required was for the judges to make it official.

That evening we had out of town friends for dinner. Usually I let my husband, Pat, read over the gems of wisdom (our entries) before I lick the envelope and send them on their merry way to impress the judges. That evening I was in a *show and glow* mood for I was quite proud of Dike's originality, sincerity, aptness of thought and clarity of presentation, (rules the entry would be judged on). I just had to share it with our guests. I asked if they would care to have a sneak preview of a winning entry that would win our son a trip to Washington. At first they thought I was kidding. After reading it I could see they were impressed.

When one of the guests handed the copy back to me he asked, "Say this is terrific . . . but how can you be so certain that it will win a trip?"

Honestly, one can get a bit weary with all the Doubting Thomases floating around. I hope for your sake there are not too many in your environment.

Had I been a gamblin' woman I would have made a bet. Instead I said, "Give Dike your address and he can drop you a card while he is in Washington."

I'll never do that again because it appeared that I might know the judges or have some pull, and it could arouse suspicion. So that's a NO NO: Braggin' before Baggin' . . . remember that.

Dike was notified he won the trip four weeks later. He brought home many interesting experiences that he shared with us. This was his first trip without the family. I sent a newspaper story of Dike's trip win to our guests.

"Anything he can do, I can do better," was now younger son Chris' attitude. He had an opportunity to prove his creativity shortly. A popcorn company was sponsoring a contest for children and asking children under 14 years of age to draw an original picture of a popcorn man. Top prize was a free trip to the New York World's Fair for a child and one adult. Besides the expense-paid plane fare, and three days' stay at a downtown hotel, the winner would also receive $150.00 for extras. My, what an exciting opportunity. I'd get to go to the fair with him! Things were poppin' and plenty of "corny" ideas "popped" forth and were discarded but when the nitty gritty time came to concentrate on one idea, we came up with a winner. It was one of the three top winners in the nation. So we saw the World's Fair in 1964.

"Can you top this?" was then Chris' challenge upon his return from the World's Fair adventure.

"Give me time, little brother," was Dike's reply.

Then it appeared on the scene . . . a trip just geared for Dike. He was to graduate from high school in June of 1968. A month before school closed the contest appeared. Ninety youths would be given the opportunity to tour Europe for six weeks. They would hostel all over the continent in remote villages, by plane, train, boat and cycle.

The Wrangler Jean Company was sponsoring this one. The requirements were to write in 50 words why you felt you would be a Good Will Ambassador in Europe. He wrote his entry, then immediately got ready to travel by getting his passport and required shots. (When I say we are positive, I also mean we are prepared).

A day before graduation he received the wire. He was on the winning team. The experience and the tour is still considered one of the special events in his life. He still corresponds with several youths he met on the excursion.

Upon his return as Dike was sharing his travelogue and showing us slides of the places he had visited, Chris announced, "Say that sounds exciting, it's my turn to go to Europe next summer".

A Clearasil Contest made it possible for his wish to be fulfilled. The next July he was jetting to Europe on what he called a trip where only the elite meet, greet and eat. It was first class all the way. He claimed he had never seen such plush places and had such exotic food.

This particular contest was a sweepstake. The number of entries in this type of contest are fantastic. It was announced that some have drawn as high as 300,000 entries. Only 30 youths — 15 girls and 15 boys — were selected. He, too, had his passport and required shots in readiness prior to the official notice of the win. If you've got a positive attitude

. . . flaunt it. But only in the family environment (for your sake).

As I stated earlier all five Hadsells were in the act of winning contests and using a positive attitude.

Daughter, Pam, had her place in the fun also. Her interest slanted toward recipes and art entries. She won cash prizes for submitting recipes in numerous national as well as local contests. It was one of her entries that won for the family a complete home library consisting of the 15-volume set of Childcraft and the 20-volume World Book Encyclopedia.

In an art contest, it was her talent that snagged for us a stereo-record unit and she supplied us with radios with her endeavors in creativity. She, at one stage of the fun and game contest pursuits, declared after winning 5 pairs of roller skates, "I get the impression I'm spinning my wheels."

After submitting an entry and winning an elaborate electric train set for the boys, we offered encouragement by telling her she really was on the "right track".

CHAPTER III

All Things Come to Him Who Waits

One year, before the Christmas HoliDAZE, my husband asked what I wanted for Christmas. At the time I needed an electric frypan. I already was enjoying a steam iron, thanks to Proctor; new toaster from generous Sunbeam; a new coffee pot presented to me from Corning Ware; and an electric blanket compliments of G.E. O yes, I also had an electric knife, can opener, mixer and toothbrushes from other sponsors.

I told the dear boy not to buy a frypan as I was positive I'd be winning one shortly. In the past month I'd entered a number of contests with priority on that particular win.

When Christmas Eve gift opening time arrived, the big square box under the tree contained an electric frypan. My husband had bought one for me.

Between January 1-20 I received letters from three different contest sponsors all congratulating me on my winning their prize of an electric frypan. How wonderful I was now able to give them as gifts to the family.

In the spring of '64 I had the inclination to remodel my kitchen. I was giving all the cabinets a fresh coat of pale yellow paint. One morning after the mail delivery I was leafing through a magazine and enjoying my morning coffee. There it was . . .

on page 32. The Westinghouse Contest display.
Amid all the appliances pictured I could see the
stately coppertone stove—a perfect addition and a
must for my kitchen redecorating project. Somehow
my 8-year-old white stove had served its purpose and
now looked ancient. I knew I could contribute it
to the church auction sale and it would raise funds
for their projects. So I neatly and discreetly mentally
found the perfect place for it.

Fifteen hundred prizes were offered in the Westinghouse contest. The first ten prizes were complete
laundry units. The second prizes were refrigerator-
freezer units, then 10 third prizes of colored stoves.
Other prizes were portable TV's and small appliances.

I disregarded all the prizes but the stove. The
rules said to write a 25-word statement on why
you liked Westinghouse products. I was so enthused
I submitted five entries that evening. This time I had
a long wait because I entered immediately. Usually
a contest is advertised and promoted several months
before the deadline. After the closing date there is a
period of from two to six weeks longer before winners
are notified. In the meantime I sewed curtains for
the kitchen windows, installed new flooring and every-
time I looked at my stove I visualized a new stream-
lined coppertone one in its place.

At this time I was acquainted with a number of
people whose hobbies were contests. We would share
ideas, discuss contests and where one might be able
to find blanks. We even formed a club that met
once a month so we could encourage one another.

One day about five weeks after the contest closed, a friend called to inform me she had just been notified that she was a winner of a portable TV. Later I heard from a number of Westinghouse winners in the area. Meanwhile I hadn't heard a thing. I assumed my timing was off, but regardless of Westinghouse I definitely would have that stove in my kitchen. I was so positive I could almost touch it. That is how vivid and real it had become to me. I kept thinking of the phrase . . . *"Thoughts are Things"*. I was convinced that if enough positive mental energy is sent out, things eventually manifest in the physical. Another phrase that is most comforting and one which should be incorporated in your thinking is . . . *"Anything the Mind Can Conceive — and Believe — It Can Achieve."* I was out to prove it to myself again, once more.

In the middle of that week, I received a legal size envelope with a congratulatory letter, and a check for $1,000. I was a second prize winner in a spray paint contest that offered all prizes in money. Talk about being elated! Don't you see — here was my stove with money to spare?

When I get excited the first thing I do is call my husband to share my enthusiasm. My opening statement usually is, "You'll never believe this . . ."

His answer usually is "Try me kid . . . I haven't heard it all yet".

I bought the coppertone stove and had it installed the following day.

I was so pleased with Project Stove, you would have thought it had dropped from outer Olympus.

Ten days later I received another letter. This one was from Westinghouse. It seems that in the process of awarding prizes, someone had overlooked sending me a notification of my third prize win, a stove. Truly I was so stunned, if one is ever able to become unglued this could have been the perfect time. The district manager called me several days later to ask when he could have the stove delivered.

I explained my recent stove purchase, "No, I didn't get the Westinghouse brand. I'd run into a clearance sale of stoves at Sears almost like the Westinghouse model, and I was able to save $85.00 below the usual cost".

The district manager was most kind and understanding. If I had purchased the Westinghouse brand, the full retail price would have been reimbursed. That is how I obtained a new washer-dryer unit . . . in lieu of a stove. Now that wasn't too dramatic because I hadn't really given a washer-dryer unit any consideration.

One week-end we went to the Texas State Fair in Dallas. I became intrigued with the color TV's. My, what sharp, colorful clear crisp pictures. That's when I got the notion what our next project would be to win . . . a color TV. I gathered all the positive thinking I could conjure up, turned on the imagining faculty and replaced our then 21-inch TV unit with a color set. I discussed our next project with the family and they all agreed COLOR TV FOR 603 (that was our house number) and easy to mentally think about when TV entered our mind.

Then it happened—our first TV win. Chris won

a 16 inch portable black and white set for naming a duck in a children's contest. About three weeks later I won a 14 inch portable TV in a local radio contest. That, too, was black and white. We now kidded one another and discussed that perhaps we were not concentrating on COLOR enough. So we agreed to give COLOR more thought.

The next opportunity that presented itself was a caption contest. In ten words we were to tell what a baby was saying. One of the newspapers was sponsoring this contest for humor. The only prizes offered were color TV's and portable sets of black and white. This time I was so positive I would win.

Of course I did . . . but alas another black and white set. I refused to be discouraged at what one might consider a failure and I would not give up. It got to be a big joke around the Hadsell house, mother is COLOR BLIND or she isn't COLOR conscious. After two years of projecting for color TV, I gave in and shelled out and purchased a color set.

The following January my husband flew to California on business. He wanted me to accompany him so we could see some live TV shows. Sounded like great fun. We did have a fun time over the weekend as we attended a number of live shows. On Monday while he was transacting business I had a free day. I chose to go to NBC studio in hopes of having the opportunity to see or talk to Art Linkletter.

May I go off on a tangent and explain why I wanted to again meet Mr. Linkletter? The year we won the family trip to Disneyland I extended for a few days my visit. A former neighbor had moved to sunny California and invited me to stay on, visit and be her guest. Here was an opportunity to see some of the TV shows.

I had watched the Art Linkletter show on occasion, and always found the program to be sincere, wholesome and entertaining. I also had hopes of one day being on a program. (A female characteristic of mine . . . I'm a show-off).

My friend was able to acquire tickets and the night before I was to visit the studio and watch the show in progress, I had a very vivid dream. I saw Mr. Linkletter choosing me from a vast audience and inviting me to be on his program. Most interesting . . . because that is exactly how it happened.

After the audience was seated prior to the program, I was waiting for my dream to unfold. Mr. Linkletter came on stage, he looked over the audience and walked up to me and questioned . . . "Don't I know you?"

Guess I was speechless for a moment because it was happening just like I had seen it in my dream.

"No, this is my first trip to Hollywood," I replied.

He asked if I would like to have a very special Christmas present. But natch . . . I was then escorted into the spotlight and a huge box was placed before me. I was to open it so home viewers and audience could see my present. Well . . . it was quite a surprise. When I raised the lid out jumped a little ole Santa Claus and scared the YELL out of me. After regaining my composture, jack-out-of-the-box presented me with a beautiful watch. The program was aired on Christmas day so all my family and friends were able to witness my TV debut.

I was now a celebrity. After the program Mr. Linkletter came to where I was seated and again asked if I was sure we had never met before today? Since that episode in '63 I have done quite a bit of research and reading on telepathy, projection in dreams and regression on past experience of ancestors, etc. I thought it would be interesting to get Mr. Linkletter's views on the subject. I, however, did not have the opportunity during my last visit. Perhaps one day I might have the occasion . . . I hope so.

Now let's pick up the story I was sharing with you earlier . . . about visiting the NBC studio. While taking the studio tour, I noted a line forming at the side of the building. People were waiting to be admitted into the studio to view a show being taped.

I asked how I could be admitted and found myself in line with the waiting group. The name of the show was *"It's Your Bet."* They were going to shoot five half-hour programs that day. One could be eligible for prizes if (No. 1) you were chosen by the camera that zoomed into the audience and stopped on you. (No. 2) If the celebrity that was playing the game, ('twas sort of like ESP) would in sequence correctly answer three questions his mate had already submitted to the MC that was conducting the show. If all answers were correctly given by the game participants, the audience player would receive the prize flashed on the board prior to the game. It could be a refrigerator, color TV, washer, etc., but it would be a major appliance. If they missed one, the prize would be of considerably lesser value, a portable appliance. If none were answered correctly that would be your prize . . . nothing.

It sounded interesting and I had nothing to do until 5 p.m. when I was to meet my husband.

While waiting, I became acquainted with a mother and daughter who were standing in line ahead of me. They began discussing the possibility of being chosen for one of the prizes. They informed me that they had been entering contests for years and had yet to win one prize.

As I listened to their failures, I realized why they hadn't won. It was obvious . . . sure they wanted to win, but instead of being positive they had doubt. Not negation or pessimism, but just enough doubt that they nullified any positive energy they might have had when they entered a contest.

(I call your attention to this because this is what most people are guilty of doing. They say they are positive . . . but somehow they don't retain this powerful energy constantly until their wishes or desires manifest).

Here was a perfect opportunity for a positive experiment. I wanted these lovely people to win their desires. The mother wanted a color TV and the daughter expressed a desire for a refrigerator. Then I turned on full-blast how great positive thinking was and asked if they would like to play a game as I wanted to prove that they could win.

They agreed but I could sense they were thinking —"What have we here, a kook?"

In all fairness I must admit the studio audience was not too large. If I had to estimate I would say about 45 to 50 people. So that was cutting the odds considerably. I told them to be passive and not project any positive energy until the item they wanted was flashed on the screen, then to know they would be chosen by the house camera, then to vie for the prize and be the winner of that prize.

They agreed. After being chosen they were to look at the answers given by the partner playing the game, then mentally project the answer to the person that was to give the correct answer. In other words, just simply play mental telepathy. I reassured them several times it was a game, and if the three of us followed the positive rules, they would win their prizes.

Then the fun and games began. The first prize which was projected on the board was a silver service with an assortment of wine and a year's supply of the wine. We knew that was not wanted, so we showed no concern. The next prize for the person in the audience to win, was a color TV. I could see both of them perk up. The next minute the house camera zoomed in on the mother. You better believe she was startled. She turned to give me a weak smile as if saying, "Well . . . I'll . . . be." The players on the stage did their part. I'm sure both mother and daughter mentally sent the answers to the person playing, and of course I did. For all three questions were correctly answered.

The bewitched, bothered and bewildered home-maker from Ohio won her first prize, a color TV. The games went on and prizes of no importance were offered. We then were informed there would be an hour break for lunch. The show would be continued after lunch, as three more programs had to be taped. The three of us went across the street for a bite to eat. That is when the daughter asked the question I knew she was quite concerned about. Didn't I think the whole thing was a coincidence? I agreed that it certainly did seem that way. So, would she like to now win her refrigerator by coincidence?

"Why, yes let's try it again," she replied.

When we returned to the studio the crowd had tripled in size. When she observed this, one could sense she was concerned, then she relaxed. The first prize that flashed on the screen for the audience to vie for was her refrigerator. The person that the camera zoomed in on was none other than she. Briefly she was startled then she relaxed to play the game. When the mental telepathy game began it was amusing how swiftly the players picked up the answers. But of course, she was the winner of a refrigerator. Well . . . what do you know, another coincidence? Perhaps.

After the show was completed a 10 minute break was called before taping the next program. The mother and daughter then approached me and asked what it was that I wanted to win. I replied, "Would you believe, not a thing?"

I had the satisfaction of proving to them how powerful positive thinking is. They then left.

The Name It and Claim It Game

I still had two hours to spend before meeting my husband, so I stayed to continue the game. I had meant it when I said there was nothing I wanted or needed.

As I watched the proceeding I could also sense the audience. There wasn't a single positive person in the whole crowd. I remembered my dear old mother had mentioned several times in her letters that some day she would like to have a color TV. So here I go again. The camera now zoomed on me. The correct answers were sent to the players. I will admit I got a little concerned for a moment when one of the players was wanting to give the wrong answer. Sigh . . . he paused then came forth with the right answer. Thanks to the lovely people on the panel my mother is now enjoying a color TV.

Why that's witchcraft . . . some of you might be surmising. Why of course it's not . . . let's call it WISHcraft. But let's analyze this situation. The prizes were there for anyone that wished for them. The players of the game have free will. They could accept or reject anything that was mentally suggested to them.

Question No. 1. What if several people were vying for the same prize; which one would be the winner?

Answer: The one that emitted the most positive energy.

Question No. 2. Can anyone do this?

Answer: It is being done every day in every way. It's about time you are made aware of it.

When I became aware of the powerful tool one

has when using their mind with control, I incorporated into my consciousness this phraseology. "I will always use my power of the mind for constructive, creative purposes, for everything that is good, honest, pure, constructive and humanitarian. I will never use these powers of the mind for anything that is destructive or harmful to anyone. If that be my intention I will not be able to function with these powers."

This I am most sincere about, for in my continuing research I am aware that this powerful energy can be channeled for physical healings, to encourage the depressed, and can be of benefit for anyone who asks for help.

CHAPTER IV

Yes . . . You Can

"I'm curious to find out if a pooped couple with 3 kids can recapture the rapture of springtime ecstasy in their fat, forty, frustrated years?"

This is the entry I submitted in every contest that was offering a trip to Europe. I'd set my sights to high-fly, and vie for a trip to Paris, France.

I began project-Paris — the first of the year. I was anticipating celebrating my 40th birthdate in Paris. I would be 40 years old on June 1 of that year.

Back as far as I can remember I'd heard how picturesque, romantic and exciting Paris is. Sidewalk cafes, music, relaxed friendly happy people. That's what prompted me to write the above entry for I wanted to go see for myself. Of course, my husband would accompany me. You know it takes two. A he and a she.

I really was curious to find out if one could recapture the rapture of springtime ecstasy in the city of life, love and the pursuit of something!

I realize now that anything one does is based on what one thinks; how much daydreaming or energy one projects toward their goal. In fairness I must admit at the time of my project "Paris", I was impressed and influenced by all the things I'd heard and read about it. So I had already half-way convinced myself it could happen. Now all I needed was to get the body there to experience in the flesh, if you will, that it could be done.

I could go into a long declaration on what my idea of ecstasy means. Suffice it to say a carefree, comfortable, cozy, cool, calm and protected feeling. That, dear reader, is my idea of ecstasy.

A cola contest began shortly after the first of the year. It was just the contest I had been watching for. Top prizes were trips to anywhere in the world you wanted to go. The promotion layout had this question: "Where in the World do you want to go and why?" I knew I wanted to go to Paris, I knew why I wanted to go and I knew I was going to Paris.

I was not too concerned about which contest would make this possible. Perhaps it would come in the form of a sum of money, but this time I would wait until my target date, June 1, then purchase the tickets.

When you win trip prizes they usually are package deals and must be accepted and taken by the winner.

I was not too concerned where in Europe any contest would specify, because once I was in Europe, there would be no problem flying into Paris. So I decided I would enter every contest until I won, and I had six months to make this dream a reality.

I'd read some place that the stronger your faith, the more power you have. Also, one should continue to use your "God-power" within you and you acquire more power. "You do not use up God-power", the statement said. "It is inexhaustible, like the air we breathe".

In recent years I have been asked a number of

34

times by students who are following the Eastern philosophy and vying toward "Spiritual Growth", did I not feel I was misusing "God-power" for material things? Also they claimed if I continued to use this power I would lose it.

My answer to this question must come from my experience. I do not believe it is a misuse of mental power to desire material things. Nor do I feel that it is "God's Will" to punish anyone with pain, disease and poverty. Perhaps I have a different God than people who have this belief. To my way of thinking I like the phrase: "Ask and you shall receive, Knock and it shall be opened unto thee, Seek and you will find." I have yet to come across any restrictions that limit you by saying . . . "but don't ask for a trip, health, or a better job".

If your way of thinking puts the damper on this type of goal or desire, then, dear reader, that is only your concept. I could write several novels on the misconceptions people have due to environment, religious dogma, guilt feelings and set ways in their thinking. It is not my intention to condemn their thinking but I do say if they have reached a point of "No Return" and they ponder or look for reasons, they must surely come up with the fact that they must change their ways. To change your ways you must change your thinking.

There I go again sandwiching in a sermonette in one of my fun and game projects. My son keeps a soap box available for jest when I become "sermonnettish."

Do let's get on with the Paris project.

I want you to know the cola contest to which I submitted my entry did not award me a trip to Paris. They did, however, present me with a third prize — a Hammond Electric Organ. I did some serious thinking on that win. Here is the explanation I feel may have prompted the organ win.

Judges are nice people. Some are serious, some possess humor, and some have sympathy. I base this on the type of entries I've submitted and won with in the past. One sometimes can write sad, glad, bad and sometimes a little "mad".

When the judges in the cola contest read my entry I'm sure they found originality, aptness of thought and clarity of presentation or it would not have been considered one of the top major prizes. However, I feel when it came to the final judging, the group talked it over and were concerned I might be a bit "mad" or be disappointed if they sent me to Paris and I didn't recapture the rapture. Perhaps they surmised what I really needed was therapy and what better way to get it . . . than to play the organ? Could this be the reason why they awarded me the organ? I'll never know, but I can guess, can't I.

Now surely you don't think I was disappointed . . . . remember earlier I said there was never failure . . . only delay in results. This is how I felt about this contest.

As I stated there are so many contests going on all the time, but I was only interested in trips to Europe or cash award contests, so I continued to enter.

The next contest that interested me was sponsored

by a men's sportswear company. They were only offering 6 prizes. Six trips to major cities in Europe. Rules were to complete in 25 words or less, what city in Europe you would like to go to.

I again submitted I wanted to go to Paris and why. Also I submitted another entry that I wanted to go to Venice, Italy. It was beyond Paris and prize-wise it was the best deal one could win. The trip was first class but for only one person.

On May 15th of that year we still had not heard of any trip win. I'd won a number of minor prizes but no trip. We did get our shots and passports and we also questioned what was taking somebody, somewhere so long to notify us.

On May 23 we heard about our son, Chris winning his New York trip for two. We were quite elated as we realized New York is half way to Europe from Texas. We had only 8 days left until the June 1st target date.

On May 29th we got the telegram from the men's sportswear contest. My husband had won the trip to Venice, Italy. He could leave immediately if he wished.

We did some wheelin' 'n dealin' changing the first class tickets to tourist class and we were actually refunded money from the airline after booking passage for two. It worked out beautifully.

Chris, my husband and I flew to New York, spent three days at the World's Fair and went on to Europe after we saw Chris on a plane back to Texas.

Now I want all of you to know . . . YES . . . you can recapture the rapture of springtime ecstasy although fat, forty and frustrated. When our exciting trip (three weeks in length) to the enchanting cities in Europe came to a close, I again felt thirty, pretty and flirty.

So it's a state of mind . . . I agree. But please don't knock it until you've tried it.

CHAPTER V

Now Act Surprised . . . They Expect It

Little did I realize what was in the making for taking when I went to the contest club meeting of which I was a member.

The group met the first Monday in September shortly after I returned from my European tour.

I was now known as "The Gad About" with the many trips I'd won in the contesting field. I might add I also was glad-about the many comforts and conveniences the merchandise prizes I had won provided.

"Can you top this?" seemed to be the question that now presented itself.

After I shared my trip experience with the members present, everyone expressed a desire that they, too, might win a trip to Europe.

When the announcement was made of current contests now in progress, I really perked up when I heard the Formica Company was awarding a $50,000 home in their building material promotion. Now to me that would be "The livin' beginning".

The Formica home that someone would win had been on display at the New York Wold's Fair. I must admit, although I attended the fair I was not aware of the contest nor their display. Perhaps I was too excited about our European tour.

The contest was promoting Formica products. All

home-builders in the USA who built a home with a certain amount of Formica products, and who participated in the Parade of Homes, had the entry blanks and the rules stated.

In order to participate in the contest, the rules specified you had to be a family homeowner and you must have visited one of the Formica homes participating in the contest. The deadline was on Friday of this particular weekend and it was then Monday evening. I was told the only Formica home participating in the area that had blanks for the contest was in Garland, Texas, nineteen miles from Irving.

On the way home from the club meeting that evening I kept thinking of the house, all new . . . modern . . . spacious. The more I thought about it the better I liked the idea.

Tuesday morning when I woke up, all I thought about was the house. After my husband left for work and the children were off to school I tried to get with my daily tasks. Call it hunch . . . intuition, or WISHcraft I felt compelled to drive to Garland to register in the sweepstake.

It began to rain. I called a friend who also enjoys entering contests and happens to live in Irving. I asked her to drive to Garland with me to register.

"Sorry I can't go Helen, I just washed my hair and it's a miserable day to be on the highway today."

I called another friend in hopes she might go with me. No, she was sewing and didn't want to get out in the rain. She reminded me that the contest promotion had been on for almost 2 years and it was a waste of gas and time at this late date. I then tried to bribe her into going with me by telling her I would buy her a pizza for lunch if she would accompany me. No success.

Next I tried to talk myself out of going until later in the week . . . but I certainly did not dismiss the idea of entering. Somehow the most important thing for me to do that day was to get in the car, drive to Garland and register my name for that home.

I drove in the rain, located the Formica home, registered both my name and my husband's name. I then sat in the spacious living room as I admired the beautiful furnishings and mastercraft workmanship of the Formica features.

It was then I became aware I would win the house . . . Don't ask me how . . . I just knew.

I took an entry blank home and was rereading the rules when I pushed a panic button. I'd signed my husband's name and the rules stated the winner must have visited one of the Formica homes. He hadn't.

Do you know I insisted that he must drive to Garland with me and familiarize himself with the house so when the judges notified us we would not be disqualified by not following the rules. I am a *stickler* for following rules of a contest. Since I learned you can lose a major prize by goofin' and not following the rules.

I know a woman who entered a contest to win a five room house of furniture. She really wanted and needed the prize because they were then building a new home. She signed her 11 year old daughter's name to the entry she submitted. When the judging firm called and the daughter answered and told the judges she was 11 years old, that was the end of that win. The mother later called the agency to explain she hadn't noticed the contest was for adults over 21 years of age. The judges were sorry she overlooked that rule but they had to abide by rules as the furniture company sponsoring the contest would not award their top prize to an 11 year old.

That same week-end we drove to Garland, introduced ourselves to the builder and reviewed the details of the house. When we returned home my great expectations began to manifest. Active faith alone, will impress the subconscious and I wasn't going to miss a bet.

The following week I decided the house would be furnished with hand carved Spanish furniture. I'd seen just what I wanted on one of our trips to Mexico. I asked my husband to draw up plans for the house. The boys also put in their wants and desires. They suggested we have a huge game room; one that would accommodate a full size pool table; the organ we had won earlier, the TV center and music area and several couches for informal entertaining. I expressed the desire that the kitchen and breakfast area be open to a patio garden. We got so specific we were all projecting toward its reality.

Our next act of faith was to spend week-ends looking at lots for the house to be built on. The rules stated we could choose a lot anywhere in the United States and Formica would pay for the lot too. We spotted three lots that would have suited our purpose. We had a fun time on this project.

Six weeks passed and still no news. Then one evening while I was attending a club meeting the phone rang. My husband was there to answer it.

The firm that was handling the contest promotion called. No, not to say we had won any prize—just to ask questions. The formal procedure is to see if contestants followed all the rules.

Question No. 1. "Was H. B. Hadsell married and a home owner?"

Question No. 2. "Did we visit a Formica home and where?" Of course my husband could answer all the questions because we had followed the rules.

This preliminary investigation does not mean that you have won a prize. We were informed this is necessary to avoid awarding top prizes to people who are not eligible by some rules not followed. When a major prize of that nature is awarded, the company must be certain that there is such a person.

We were excited after the investigation and now questioned ourselves how long it would take them to make it official that we were the winners of their home.

A week later, on a Friday morning to be exact, I announced that we would hear of our house win today. I recall commenting on how I better get the house straightened up early, in case the officials came early. Too, I'd have to make a trip to the bakery to get pastries to serve these lovely people. My husband decided to stay home from work that day so he could be on hand for the big moment.

At 3 p.m. the phone rang. The person on the other end of the line identified himself as one of the "big wheels" from Formica. Heavens no, he didn't refer to himself as a "big wheel" . . . but logic will tell you they certainly would not send a "nobody" for a big deal like awarding a $50,000 house. He also was accompanied by a public relations man whom I can only refer to as a ball-of-fire and a "most jet-up and go-blow and show individual". I really liked the fellow because it's the live wires that get a job done.

The "big wheel" asked if he and one of his associates (the ball-of-fire) might come to our home to discuss a contest prize for which we were being considered. "If your husband is not home this time of the day, we will wait until later in the evening as we wish to have both of you present", he explained.

I almost blew it . . . for I was about to blurt out . . . "What took you so long?" Instead I answered, "Oh, do come on out, my husband is home today and I have the coffee perkin'."

"Now act surprised, they expect it", was the instruction I gave my husband.

They came . . . We did.

When the glad tidings were verbally made official, the merry-go-round began. They informed us that there had been over 2 million entries in the contest.

It took no time to get the home ready for the show. They approved of the lot, selected the architect, incorporated our wishes in the home plans. The Formica team, the builder and everyone connected with the Hadsell house were livin' dolls. They did so many nice "added things" to please us. Now every time I see any Formica products I again mentally thank this team of lovely people for turning our wishes into reality.

What about taxes is the first question people seemed to ask.

Formica thought of that too. They informed us if there was any financial concern over taxes, they would help us with this so we would not be burdened by turmoil, taxes and turn against this good fortune. However, we were able to take care of the situation and for the past five years we have enjoyed our spacious, gracious, comfortable Formica fortress.

One of the nicest features about this beautiful home is the carefreedomness of work, worry or waxing. Formica took care of us and now Formica takes care of itself.

Beautiful people, are you beginning to realize the power of positive thinking and active faith?

Change your expectancies and you change your conditions. Begin to act as if you expected success, happiness and abundance; *prepare for your good.*

Nothing is too good to be true, nothing is too wonderful to happen, nothing is too good to last; when you have a positive attitude for your good.

CHAPTER VI

How To Be Successful
Without Really Trying

Following are a number of personal experiences to again relay what can happen when the ideas of security, health, happiness and abundance are established in the subconscious.

It means a life free from all limitation! It surely must be the Kingdom which Jesus spoke of, where all things are automatically added unto us. I say automatically added unto us, because all life is vibration: and when we vibrate to success, happiness and abundance, the things which symbolize these states of consciousness will attach themselves to us. In other words, "tune in".

Feel rich and successful and suddenly you receive a gift or large sum of money.

My husband and I attended a company Christmas party where a door prize of a tape recorder would be presented in a drawing. Everyone in attendance had heard of our phenomenal success in winning things. One man, prior to the drawing jokingly announced. "The Hadsells should be disqualified because nobody can win when they enter a contest."

Of course, we won the tape recorder . . . and we didn't even try.

Why did we win? Perhaps our past culmination of

positive energy had something to do with the win. I recall the incident quite clearly. When we were aware what the door prize was I simply expressed a desire that I might win it, for we had intentions of getting one as a gift for one of the children.

For this incident I have no logical explanation except to say . . . 'twas just plain ole WISHcraft.

If you should happen to be resentful and envious, (and admit it to yourself) take the powerful positive statement. "What God has done for others he now does for me and more!" Repeat it until it becomes like second nature in your consciousness. Then all the things you desire will come your way. Don't be discouraged if you have a desire (as I mentioned in the above personal experience) and it does not produce results as swiftly as the tape recorder win. Remember there is never any failure . . . only a delay in results.

Over the years I have learned not to be too disappointed in anything, anyone, or any goal I project. If it does not manifest as fast as I might wish it to . . . say for example . . . I had not won the tape recorder, my attitude would have been . . . oh well, you win some you lose some. I KNOW it was premature but it is coming to me.

Don't ever dismiss or nullify good positive energy because you are disappointed. Acquire the attitude . . . guess I need a little more patience. It really does wonders for your peace of body, mind and well being. You *will get it*.

Somewhere I read this bit of advice that I find most apropos. "No man gives to himself, but himself, and no man takes away from himself, but himself: The 'Game of Success' is a game of solitaire, as you change, all conditions will change."

MY SOW AND REAP PHILOSOPHY

Nine area automobile dealerships and super market food companies co-sponsored a contest. One had to go to the auto showroom to view the largest model car that was filled to capacity with groceries. The person that guessed closest to the amount of the total sum of groceries would win a $150.00 coupon book which could be spent in the stores. Second closest guess would win the use of a sport car for a week.

When I heard of this contest I called a friend and asked her if she would like to accompany me to play the guessing game and win some groceries.

We began our "fun and game" day this way. Our first visit to the dealer we submitted our guesses and agreed that I had the correct sum and I would win the $150.00 prize in that dealership. Our next stop we jokingly designated that my friend would win the cash award at that dealer. The next place I would win and the next one she would win.

I must again repeat we were in a very gay mood and had great fun playing the game of guessing.

There were four places where I would win the first prize and four places where she would win. When we came to the ninth dealer she suggested, "Let's win for my neighbor, who has five children, and really could use the $150.00 grocery money. We submitted our guesses in her neighbor's name and concluded our "fun and game" day.

Winners would be announced the following Saturday. We stayed home that day to answer the phone when the dealers would notify the winners.

One might, at this point say, "This is unreal," but let me assure you it is fact.

I had three phone calls that afternoon. Two informed me that I won their prize of a $150.00 coupon book. One told me I missed by 3 cents, but I won the second prize, the use of their sport car for a week.

My friend won the $150.00 prize at two dealers and the neighbor whose name we submitted also won the first prize of $150.00 from another dealer. The one dealer I hadn't heard from concerned me. I told my friend I had a hunch he was dishonest because I was certain I had submitted the right guess at that dealership. The more I thought of it the more I felt compelled to follow my hunch and check up.

On Monday I called the place and asked the secretary who answered the phone, "Who won the $150.00 grocery certificate book?" She told me the supervisor who was in charge of the promotion had taken care of that and she felt the winner had already been notified.

I told her I would call back and speak to the supervisor as I was most interested in who won the prize. Several hours later I again called. This time I spoke to the man in charge. He informed me the winner had been notified but he forgot his name. It was somewhere on his desk and he had a customer so he had no time to look it up. I told him I would call back in an hour as I was curious to find out who won. At this point I felt certain that this man was dishonest and I knew I would not drop the issue. When I called again he curtly informed me a Mrs. Helen Hadsell was the winner and she had been notified. Then I replied, "How wonderful; I know her. I'm so pleased to hear she won."

What choice did he now have but to follow through?

Two days later in the mail I received the prize of a $150.00 coupon book with a note of this nature. "We are pleased to inform you that you are the winner in our contest." The postmark on the envelope indicated it was mailed after my telephone conversation.

The moral of this experience is: I did not entertain any negative ideas about anyone being dishonest, etc. but when the strong hunch prompted me to investigate I did and I was correct.

In my experience of contesting, I have had only two instances when I felt the person in charge was not honest. Both were in local promotions.

It now is amusing to me when I think about dishonesty. For, "As you sow . . . so shall you reap." The more I become aware of this well organized universe we live in, the more I realize the perfection of this law. You really don't kid anyone but yourself when you are dishonest. Although at the time you may feel you have pulled a fast one, sometime in the future someone will pull a fast one on you. This law was laid down for us many centuries ago.

This raises the thought . . . Perhaps you are

reaping what you once sowed; perhaps the reason the prize was withheld is for this law to be balanced for one of the past shenanigans you pulled. This is very possible, but again, I could only follow my intuition and pursue the incident to my satisfaction or dismiss it as not worth the effort.

I'm using the "Grow As I Go Plan" for I realize if I were perfect I certainly would not be on this planet, earth, learning and overcoming my past boo-boos.

Perhaps this is why I find life so exciting and beautiful. I have no friends or enemies . . . only teachers in this classroom of learning.

CHAPTER VII

Hunches Are The Handiest Things

After we moved into our $50,000 home we had no more reason "to keep up with the Joneses" . . . we were the Joneses.

My son Chris, at that time 16 years old—a card . . . the joker—called my attention to the fact that he at long last was in the surroundings he should have been accustomed to a long time ago. In other words . . . what took you so long? He now expressed a desire for a sport car, a "sharp" new wardrobe, impressive rings and things to show how prosperous he was, and he wanted to create a new image . . . ok I'll say it . . . he was a show-off.

You who have teen-agers or know some, I'm sure can understand what a difficult time the little darlings can sometimes make for themselves. Seems at times no amount of love, attention, patience, and understanding can reach them during one period of the "growing . . . blowin' . . . showing syndrome". Fortunately this period is brief and one can always be comforted in the fact that—this too will pass. Again let me reassure you . . . there are never any failures only a delay in results . . . there now, does that give you hope? Anyway this was the period Chris was going through.

My psychology teacher summed it up this way in

class one evening: "Parents who have teen-agers are either crazy, stupid or gluttons for punishment." He confessed he had no choice but to go all through high-school with a bunch of teen-agers. He is a rare honest KOOK trying to figure out teen-agers he has to help and understand in one of the corrective institutions. Not only is he a staff member in the corrective institution but he also teaches an adult psychology class which I attended. I could have clued him in . . by telling him there is no way to figure them out . . . for they are like the tide, constantly changing. But who was I to tell him anything, he was my teacher and I was buckin' for a good grade in the course. (I'm working toward a degree in psychology presently . . . so I'm using psychology).

I didn't mean to get so long winded on the teenage subject . . but that might give you further verification that we are the typical family, nutty as well as fruitful.

But do let's get back to Chris' desire . . the complete list of items he was vying for. Would you now believe a contest appeared on the scene that answered all his wants?

The Union Carbide Company was sponsoring a contest for teen-agers. Rules stated for the design of a piece of jewelry that would appeal to the youth. Requirements were to use one or more Linde Star sapphires on the piece of jewelry you designed. The company was plugging star sapphires.

I understood the contest was in progress for almost six months and all art class students in the high-schools throughout the United States were informed and encouraged to submit their ideas. There were two first prizes. One for a girl and one for a boy. The big first prize included a trip to New York for a week to attend the national jewelry show. One parent could accompany "their genius child jewelry design winner". A star sapphire ring would be presented to the winner, a gold wrist watch, two pieces of luggage, a $1,000 cash award, plus a trip to the men's manufacturing firm to choose a fall wardrobe of your choice. Now I ask you . . . how does that grab you . . . for having all your (begs in one askit?) . . I mean all your eggs in one basket. Don't you see that contest was geared for Chris.

It was about the last week before the contest closed when he got all fired up about entering it.

What kind of entry wins . . . and what did he submit? Following are the incidents that led up to his win.

He discussed the ideas of the contest with the whole family one week-end and came up with this. Nearly everyone at that time in high-school was either in a band, a combo or thought they could play a musical instrument of some sort. He first toyed with the idea of submitting a banjo, but after giving it more thought he then discarded it, the reason being, if teen-agers were entering the contest somebody would surely send or think of a banjo—it was too obvious and could be duplicated.

He maintained the musical idea and then the thought came. Why not a staff with two notes and a treble clef. Why that would be a great idea for a tie bar and would appeal to all the teen-agers. Although the rules did not call for you to title the piece of jewelry you designed he figured he would call it the "LINDE GO GO" It was a natural for this entry. Now he was so excited he drew his idea on paper.

He is not artistically inclined nor was he an art student, but that was not a specific requirement. It included all high-school students. His enthusiasm now was on high. Then he yelled out . . . "I just had another great idea", as he headed for the garage and tool chest. He came back a few minutes later with a pair of pliers and a flexible piece of wire. He then commenced to shape the wire into a staff. He then made another trip for finer wire to depict the lines where the notes would be placed. He puzzled for a minute what might be suitable to represent the star sapphire that would be incorporated on the jewelry. He headed for the pantry, looked at the dried rice and bean assortment I had on hand. He decided on two small dried peas—He then glued the whole thing together, sprayed it gold except the peas which he left a pale green.

I don't mind boasting a bit here because I was quite proud of his workmanship and WINgenuity.

Although the contest called for a drawn sketch, which he did, he also felt compelled to mail in this 'paste up' idea. He mounted it in a jewelry box lined with black velvet and it looked quite impressive.

As far as I was concerned he already had a prize for the amount of pleasure he derived from his creativity.

After he mailed in his entry I then got excited about getting to go to New York again. I went shopping and bought a pale lemon colored suit for the trip, shopped for new accessories as I waited for the judges to notify him he won the first prize.

On Monday about two weeks after the contest closed I woke up that morning with the strong hunch that today would be the day we would hear from the jewelry design contest.

I was so positive I would have made a small bet on it happening. The mail man came and no news in the mail . . . but that didn't discourage me. There could still be news forthcoming via telephone or wire.

We had planned on going shopping some time that day to get Chris a pair of shoes. We had to do it before 5 p.m. as he went to baseball practice at that time. Somehow I kept postponing leaving the house . . . just like I was stalling for time. Then the phone rang . . . shortly before 4 p.m. It was one of the judges from New York. Chris answered the phone. They informed him that they only had one question to ask . . . was Chris a boy or a girl? His answer was "I'm all boy."

The next morning we received the wire that Chris won first prize for his jewelry design entry.

My hunch paid off by staying home until the phone call, as we later learned.

While we were in New York enjoying the prizes, praises and fabulous places the lovely public relations people took us to, we finally met one of the judges. (This was after the prize had been awarded). They wanted to meet the two top teen-age designers.

One of the judges, a woman, explained how difficult it was in making the top award selections. She told that there was no question about the girl winner but the final judging of the top teen boy entry proved a challenge. The final decision was between a boy named Mike who, incidentally, submitted a "banjo" as his entry, and Chris for his musical staff presentation. When the nitty gritty time came to select one winner, the judges were tired after several days of studying all the entries and it was still a tie between Chris and Mike. The woman judge wanted Chris to win because she was so impressed that a boy would go to extra trouble to submit an actual paste-up. The men judges tried to get her to agree with them and give Mike the prize because they were certain Mike was a boy and they were worried if they made it official that Chris won and he turned out to be a girl they would have problems, with two girl winners.

So they did have a consideration. The woman judge said she finally compromised to complete the judging, but on one condition. She insisted they call this kid from Texas. "If he answers the phone and tells us he is a boy he gets the prize . . . but if no one is home or answers the phone I will concede to let Mike be the winner." They agreed as they wanted to conclude their judging that afternoon.

Well Chris was home, he answered the phone, he is a boy, and he was the winner.

This incident again should convince you that when you have a hunch and it makes sense . . . follow it. In my personal experience it pays off 10 out of 10 times.

What an opportunity that was for Chris. From desiring to acquiring his wishes it only took four weeks.

This prize win and experience was another of the Hadsell hi-lights.

CHAPTER VIII

The Supreme Test

Now just what makes you think I should limit my positive thinking to contest wins? I admit I had my beginning with the will to win contest goal, but then something exciting happened to open a whole new concept for me.

Four years ago I drove to Fort Worth, Texas, at the insistence of one of my friends to hear a man from Laredo, Texas. His name was Jose Silva. Mr. Silva was lecturing on power of the mind. He told how one could control habits, weight, sleep without drugs. He offered a 48 hour course which included techniques of mental imagery for better health, better memory, superior intuition and productivity. Also how one could control habits, weight, sleep without drugs, and control pain. The man was so sincere, and as I listened to him explain one's mind potential I knew I had to take this course. Why, I got so excited I could hardly wait until the following evening to begin class training. That, dear reader, was the best investment I have ever made to date.

Four months after completing the Mind Control course I had the occasion to give the techniques I had been taught the Supreme Test.

My husband and I were involved in an automobile accident one evening on a slick sleet covered bridge. My face was thrown against the dash board as a car hit us head-on. The impact flattened my nose, caused internal facial damage and I was unable to breathe due to the great amount of blood I was swallowing. I had two choices . . . to push the panic button and bleed to death, or stop the bleeding.

Dear reader, let me now confess that in the past, I probably was one of the most difficult patients with whom the medical doctors had coped. I went into hysterics at the sight of blood. I had so many fears of dying, sickness, and pain, I frankly could have been labeled a prize neurotic nut.

I've never confessed this to anyone before . . . but I feel I should relate this incident to you to prove how one's concepts can be a detriment. When I was carrying my second child, Dike, I so dreaded delivery, and accompanying labor pains, that I delayed the big scene. I really had the "know-how" to put myself in agony. WHY? Because I didn't know any better. I was stupid. I thought you were supposed to suffer, so I did.

Seems like every time I heard some person relate their experiences of surgery or pain I incorporated it into my consciousness, HOOK . . LINE . . . AND THINKER.

Anyway, from the time of conception, a normal pregnancy is considered to be nine months. But as I confessed earlier I certainly wasn't normal; I carried the baby 11 months. The doctor finally had to force labor. When I finally played the "big scene" and the baby was born he weighed 12 pounds 8 ounces. He had hair down to his shoulders. Had he been able to speak I'm sure he would have demanded of "his keeper" a good reason for the delay! The doctor claimed it had to be a 10 or 11 month pregnancy. At that time I was extremely afraid of pain, but of course now I realize I was intensifying it with my powerful fear.

Now let's get on with the accident experience because, WOW! was I fortunate, for when it occurred, I was clued in on how to handle the situation. Thanks to the MIND CONTROL program.

One of the techniques we were taught in the Mind Control course was to stop and control bleeding and control pain.

I immediately mentally demanded the bleeding to stop . . . and do you know what? . . it did. At this point the medical doctor would claim (and rightly so) that our body has a survival mechanism that triggers and aids us to respond to survive. I agree . . but when one possesses a powerful imagination and fear, it overrides any psysiological response that would react, and one can (and many times does) bleed to death, or die of shock caused from fear and panic. I could have been one of those statistics had it not been for the Mind Control techniques of stopping the bleeding.

After forty-five minutes of lying on the car seat until help arrived, I was then placed in an ambulance which sirened all the way to the hospital to the emergency receiving unit. (I question why the BIG RUSH, for the events that followed were a farce.)

After being wheeled into the emergency room for incoming patients I lay on a cold table for an hour or more while papers had to be signed and until my turn came for a "look at". I kept my eyes closed since the flood lights I was directly under, were intense. Finally two staff members came to view my broken body. One had this to say. "I wonder what she looked like?"

I tell you this . . not to belittle the hospital system, because I'm sure the staff only do what they know—but hopefully, to help you handle a situation if you happen to be in a similar circumstance. And I hope you never are.

Again I had a chance to feel sorry for myself, rant, rave, moan and groan or control the situation by thinking positive (another supreme test.) So I began my mental musings with constructive creative thinking. "I will be fine; why, with the remarkable plastic surgery I hear they are now doing, I know they can improve on my looks . . . This body will heal itself so fast my medical case history will be a miracle for its speedy recovery." Over and over I mentally told myself the above positive suggestions.

The diagnosis of the injuries sustained from the accident after a complete once over, twice over . . . three times over (I must say when they once got around to examination, they were most thorough.) Fractured ribs in the lower back, bruised spleen, right ankle swollen three times the normal size. They could find no reason for this as there was no fracture visible in X-ray. Immediate surgery to reconstruct my nose and repair facial damage was recommended. I was given sodium pentothal to undergo face and nose surgery.

Prognosis for the damage and injury in the back, ribs and ankle would be six weeks of limited activity in a wheel chair plus wearing of a corset for back support.

After the facial surgery and upon regaining consciousness, I woke up to a room full of friends that came to bring healing energy, (they claimed). People truly are beautiful. One of my friends, a former registered nurse, insisted on just sitting beside my bed, as she claimed she could sense my physical needs and would administer to my needs until the anesthetic wore completely off and I was in control and rational.

After my system was free of the drugs administered for surgery I never had another shot or pain killing pill during the two weeks I remained in the hospital. I didn't need it. When I was aware of discomfort I merely "conned" myself by imagining the throbs of pain, (that I once was so fearful of) were healing pulsations. With each awareness of the throbbing sensation I mentally repeated . . . healing . . . healing . . . healing.

This is interesting, for this was the first time I realized the throbbing sensation that is called pain, comes in cycles and isn't constant. I also was aware that when I used the technique of physical relaxation I was taught in Mind Control, the intensity of the throbbing was very mild. I now had changed pain cycles to positive healing cycles. There was no more pain, only pleasant healing pulsations.

Ah, ha . . . I sense doubt in some of you readers. This is to be expected, for prior to my Mind Control training, I too, had been a big doubter. Some of you might call this technique self-hypnosis; some, programming, and some, plain stupidity, since drugs were available to keep me knocked out. But I will say, not one of you can say it doesn't work because I'm here to tell you it does and it did.

I must keep telling you the power of the mind is fantastic. I'm sure some of you are aware of the fire-walkers in Africa that walk over hot coals and do not get burned nor do they feel discomfort. Or of the people that are human pin cushions, and feel no pain as pins are stuck in their bodies. They have conditioned and disciplined themselves with their thinking to such a degree that they actually refuse pain. They are not special people. I certainly am not special. We all have this ability to control feelings, pain and environments and our lives. Don't limit yourself as this works in all capacities.

BIG QUESTION MARK? "But I haven't had any mental training, so how does one develop this powerful positive attitude you're talking about?" In Chapter X, *Anything I Can Do . . . You Can Do Better,* I will give you a step by step plan for positive thinking and results, but remember you must first have the desire to be master of your mind.

Scientists tell us that we are using less than 10 percent of our mind power. I believe it, because as I continue and study on mind power I am amazed at what one is capable of doing by right or by wrong thinking.

My healing was what one might term a "miracle". When I was released from the hospital and back at home, the wheel chair came home with me. Of course it served a useful purpose—I looked at it as it sat in the corner while I took over my household activities. I thought "I am not an invalid; I am in complete control of my body . . . my body does not control me . . . I control my body." and boy, did it straighten up and perform!

I was requested to check with the doctor who did the face surgery, and the doctor who was tending to my back and leg injury in about a week after being released from the hospital. I really didn't want to go, but it was required by the doctors for their reports to collect fees from the accident insurance company.

I first went to the surgeon who did such a fine job of rebuilding my nose. He was about to probe and "nose around" and check his workmanship by inserting a metal object up my nose when I rebelled. I told him I was quite happy with my nose job. I felt great—it had healed perfectly, and I had no further need for wasting his or my time. Yes, I was rude and I'm sure I hurt his pride by being so abrupt.

My policy to always"leave 'em laughing', lovin', loyal and lucky to know me" was a *bust*. I goofed miserably, so I had no choice but to make amends.

I have always been proud of having a sense of humor, although sometimes my husband disagrees with me and tells me that my humor doesn't make sense. Nevertheless I spent the next day trying to compensate for my rude behavior during my visit to the doctor. I hoped that he might have a sense of humor . . . so I pulled out my crayons (I keep on hand for my granddaughter when she comes for a visit) and I drew a beautiful picture of my nose. I then composed a citation which I typed and attached under the drawing of the nose. I framed the entire masterpiece and titled it. AWARD OF MERIT FOR DR. (and inserted his name). The citation read as follows: "After extensive nosin' around and getting this thing back in runnin' condition I am most appreciative. You have not only performed a humanitarian duty, you have definitely improved upon my beauty. All that now remains is paying through it." Then I signed my name.

Perhaps my husband was right when he said my sense of humor sometimes doesn't make sense, for I promptly received a bill for his services and I haven't seen or heard from the dear boy since.

To the readers who are inclined to agree with my husband's views that my humor doesn't make sense, that's fine. But will you give me credit on this score? I may be a nut . . . but you can bet I'll never be in a rut.

CHAPTER IX

What's Taking You So Long?

Tuesday evening May 25, 1971 Maya Perez, the well-known Psychic from Balboa, California, was in Dallas, Texas, to give a lecture on Reincarnation and Visualization. Maya is a noted lecturer as well as a psychic.

Jess Stearn's book *Door To The Future* relates some of Maya's impressions and predictions.

After a most interesting lecture a question and answer session followed. During this portion of the program Maya beckoned me from the audience to come on stage and share with the audience some of the impressions she was picking up about me. I was seated in the front row at the program. (Maya claims she picks up information about a person while being in a person's vibrations.)

Well, here we go . . . It seems the expression "nothing is hidden that shall not be revealed" comes home to me more and more as I meet with unusual psychic people.

One of the first things Maya commented on was the fact that I was in the process of losing a great deal of weight. She said I had the discipline to control the tendency to be a compulsive eater when I am frustrated.

"You accomplish nothing by continuing to blame your present obesity on emotional frustration," she stressed. "Within several months you will have a slim, trim figure." She had no way of knowing I had already begun my program of diet to lose 25 pounds, quick like, before a trip I was planning to take in August.

I admitted to Maya that I indeed, was in the process of shedding 25 pounds of excess weight. From 170 pounds (I hide my head in shame) I wanted to slim down to 140 pounds by trip time, sometime in August.

But of course I would lose the weight by trip time, and I really was pleased to hear her confirm my convictions.

For the reader who has a weight problem . . . might I share a technique that probably is the one most beneficial factor in my dieting program.

I have . . . or should I say "had" an insatiable appetite for sweets. I did fine for several days on cheese, meat and vegetables but sometimes the urge for candy became so strong I made a trip to the candy counter for chocolate-covered peanuts and ate, ate, ate until I was satisfied. That of course blew my diet. So I'm admitting I am immature and somehow need to be reminded that I am in control of the body and that the body does not control me.

The technique that reminded me I was in control of all eating goes like this: First, I made a list of the foods that tempt me. The high calorie items such as chocolate-covered peanuts, ice cream, nut brownies and caramel sauces happen to appeal to my taste buds. Second, I closed my eyes and mentally imagined I saw myself rejecting all the calorie packed goodies that were not included on my diet program. Three, rather than deprive myself and not eat when I had the craving for sweets, I mentally replaced the high calorie items with crisp carrot sticks, cool, thin cucumber slices and sweet wedges of cantaloupe. I imagined the low calorie items were much tastier than the high calorie items. In other words I was connin' myself for a calorie count down. I did this mental exercise during the day or whenever I felt tempted to those no-no calorie counters. May I say that this technique is so effective I am able to resist successfully all the foods I once craved. Today, two weeks later, I've lost 10 pounds by following my diet program. (Might I suggest that you program yourself with this technique often because what you actually are doing is replacing one habit with another and it takes repeated practice to incorporate it into your consciousness.)

There are many diets and hundreds of books written on the subject. But whatever program you happen to follow, and you have a hang-up on the sweet bit as I did . . . you better believe that this technique works.

Getting on with Maya's other impressions as she "tuned in" on me, I found this statement to be most interesting. She said I was to be a great spiritual writer . . . in fact that was my purpose this lifetime. (as I mentioned earlier she believes in reincarnation.) Fact is . . . I am presently writing a book (the one you are now reading) about my personal experiences. I found this statement doubly interesting because this is not the first time I was told I would be writing. I must share an experience that could have been responsible for planting a seed in my subconscious many years ago . . . and I am now acting upon that suggestion.

When I was 16 years old I was confined in bed for 3 months due to rheumatic fever that racked my body with pain. At that time, 1940, medical science had little to offer a person that had this serious and sometimes fatal disease. Two of my classmates also had the malady at the same time I was confined. One died of the disease, and the other boy lived five years before he too, died of heart valve damage. At that time only bed rest and pain killing drugs were the treatment to keep fever down and to dull pain.

I was brought up in a very religious church oriented environment; in fact, for 8 years I attended Parochial school taught by nuns. I went to Mass every morning, went to confession every Friday and was taught we live in sin. If we ate meat on Friday or if we missed Mass on Sunday or on a church holy day of obligation, we committed a mortal sin. I was made aware of purgatory (where one might burn in a fire until all one's sins were cleansed . . . or worse than that . . . I could go to HELL if I died with a mortal sin on my soul) Of course I swallowed all this hook . . . line and thinker. You see I didn't know any better.

I prayed, prayed and prayed to get well as I lay in bed. But there was no change. I had a perfect horror of dying because I wasn't sure about having a clean bill of thoughts to make Heaven and just the idea that I might have a mortal sin and the possibility of going to Hell or purgatory sent me into hysterics.

After three months of pain and little or no improvement, one morning I overheard the family Doctor (he made two house calls a week to look in on me) tell my mother that my heart was indicating damage and he could do very little more for me. That night I mustered up all the courage a 16-year old frightened girl can gather and I decided I wanted to die. I gave it serious thought for I was weary of constant pain, and tired of the bed. Why even if I did have to go to purgatory for a spell and get burned for a bit I could still get into heaven eventually, I told myself. Anything would be better than continuing in this situation with the outlook of death from this disease. Anyway, that is what I told myself, that the following morning I wanted to die. I just mentally set up the idea. I thought about it all night long and didn't change my mind when the light of morning appeared. That morning I verbally uttered out loud. "OK if there is a God or an angel near I want you to know I'm now ready to die. I'm tired of being in pain and not getting any better . . . so there is only one thing left, to die . . . and I don't want you to drag this out any longer, I want to die . . . do you hear me?"

Well what do you know . . . somebody heard me, or so it seemed. For as soon as I made the demand to die there appeared a rather young, serene looking man. At first I thought, "Wow, what fast service, somebody is already here to pick me up." Heavens no, I wasn't in heaven and the cool, calm, collected, young man wasn't Jesus, of that I was positive. The figure did have a rather bright yellow glow about him. He reminded me of one of the holy pictures of saints I was given by the nuns when I made good grades in school. The young man standing at the foot of my bed had such an air of peace and love radiating from him that I was startled for a moment. But I do recall that I had no fear of his presence (a man in my bedroom bit). What do you know . . . he was not there to take me away. He merely said. "What makes you think you are going to die little girl . . . you have too much to live for and too much to do."

He was real, or so it seemed to my mind's eye so I started a conversation with him. I was still determined to die, for I remember asking, "Just what can I do tied to this bed?" He then smiled and replied. "You are healed and will return to your studies. Later in life you will be inspired to write many experiences so that many will learn from you. This is the purpose for your life and you will be guided when that time comes." He then seemed to fade away as if disappearing through the wall. Well, you better believe I was one excited teen-ager. I yelled for my mother to come quickly.

After I related the experience and insisted that a man actually was here and said I was healed, she came to the bedside table, opened up the drawer, took out the thermometer to take my temperature. It happened to be normal. She then looked rather strangely at me and made me promise not to tell anyone, for it sounded crazy and was only a dream.

Thinking back at the incident, she may have been concerned that my mind was being affected by the illness.

The following morning my feet touched the floor for the first time in three months. Within the week I joined the family at the dinner table and the following week I was back in school. I pushed the incident to the back of my mind and told no one. In all the following years I never thought of the experience again. If I did, I probably promptly dismissed it.

The first of this year, 1971, I had a strong impression to write a book about my contest winning experiences, hoping it might in some way clue people in that we all have the ability to use WISHcraft. My intentions were to keep the book serious, sometimes silly and occasionally sermonettish, for that is how I express myself. I like to be sunny and punny, for as far as I'm concerned there is enough humglum, Doomsvilles U.S.A. mental energy around.

As I sat at the typewriter in my study typing my experiences for the book I kept looking at the blank wall in front of me so I could capture the appropriate words to express my thoughts.

One evening my eyes seemed to be playing tricks for I saw what appeared to be a young man. A gentle, calm, serene expression with outstretched arms and eyes turned toward the sky, he seemed to be emanating a feeling of being pleased about something. As if the flood-gates were opened, the memory and recognition of this vision rushed toward my conscious mind.

There is so much we do not yet know about the mind, memory, imagination, so at this time I have no logical explanation of what brought this about. Some might say I was hallucinating, others might think I'm illuminated and might declare me a saint. 'Tis all still a big question mark what actually happened. I will continue to seek answers to many of the questions that arise daily.

The following evening I had a repeat visit of the vision and this time I hurriedly sketched my impression of the figure on a sheet of paper. The following morning I found myself at the lumber yard buying a sheet of plywood 3 by 5 feet in size. I then stopped at an art supply shop to buy four tubes of oil paint. White, yellow, black and tan were the only colors I felt impressed to buy. I certainly am not an artist, but I had a very strong urge to try my hand at painting a study of my visitor. I got the idea to fold a double sheet of newspaper lengthwise. Taking a scissors I began cutting (sort of as I did as a child, cutting out half paper dolls then unfolding the sheet to complete the figure). The result in this instance was a silhouette of a man, halo and all. I then traced the paper figure on the board and was quite pleased with the results for it was a very good likeness of my visitor. Then the thought occurred . . . what about details such as expression of eyes, background and details. It will come . . . it will come, I kept thinking. It came.

For in three nights I had completed the painting. I even sketched in impressions of other figures

74

I had imagined I'd seen at various times in my dreams.

Teachers in the Classroom of Learning seemed to be the appropriate title for the painting. I now try to analyze if perhaps I'd seen a similar picture in one of the many museums I visited while in Europe. That might be a logical explanation how I came about painting the picture. I do so wish I had more answers, for I'm sure some of you may have had similar experiences and, too, have the question. Hopefully as time passes I might be enlightened on much of what is happening.

A most interesting incident occurred after I hung the picture. I have it displayed in a very prominent place in my home. We had guests one evening and a gentleman commented on the painting.

"Helen, no man is perfect. Yet I'm intrigued as to how perfectly you have both sides of this figure (he didn't know about my cut-out technique).

I uttered the first thought that came, perhaps in defense for I said, "What makes you think this man is in a physical body? He is perfect only to me for that is the way I saw him. Are we not all striving for perfection and balance? Perhaps if we can acquire a balance and maintain it we too, can possess a perfect physical body." You know . . . that's a good thing to strive for . . . isn't it?

'Tis interesting when Maya commented on the fact I would be doing spiritual writing. I certainly can't call this book spiritual, perhaps "spirited" might be a better word.

Maya also claimed that in one lifetime she and I

were sisters. Also that we had the same knowledge of truth.

Another interesting observation I feel I must share with you. While Maya was talking she kept stressing visualization and repeated many of the concepts I lecture on in my series of positive thinking programs.

One last comment she made. "You will be going to Egypt within several years. There you will meet two persons, I must refer to them as masters, for you will be given many answers by these masters to enable you to better understand. After meeting with the masters you will start writing in earnest with a sincere dedicated purpose."

This comment I found most interesting, for several years ago I announced to my husband that I wanted to visit Egypt and India. I even have set a date of August in 1972 to make the trip.

Now isn't life exciting when you have a vivid imagination?

In closing this chapter I must repeat . . . Anything I can do you can do better. I firmly believe it.

I recall reading, that Jesus was said to have uttered, "All these things I do . . . you can do and more." It is said that he walked on water, healed the sick, mastered bi-location and was most proficient in the practice of precipitation. (Multiplying the loaves and fishes, changing water into wine). Gads, what a challenge we are facing.

I have only one question at this time . . . What is taking us so long?

CHAPTER X

WINeuvers For WISHcraft

"I knew I was going to win," said the winner of a $10,000 first prize cash award.

So the news came as no surprise when the Dallas woman answered her doorbell and two representatives of an advertising agency were there to present her with a check for $10,000.

The story began last summer when the woman told two of her best friends, "you'd better enjoy me while you can. 1971 is going to be my year, and my whole life is going to change. Other demands will be made on my time."

Just what did she do to accomplish this WINfall? Why she used her power of positive thinking.

In her words she summed it up this way. "If you just open your heart and believe in good things — they are bound to happen. You simply train your mind to believe and to hope."

Her goal was not just $10,000. There were actually four things the woman wanted. She even set a time period that she wanted them to materialize. "1971 will be my year," she told herself.

"I needed a new car; I wanted to establish a home again with a good husband; I play the organ

77

at my church, but I never owned one of my own and I have always wanted one. And last, I wanted a little financial security and felt that $5,000 would be ample", she related.

"I made a 'wheel of fortune' . . . a simple circular piece of cardboard with cutout pictures tacked to it. There were pictures of a new automobile, a couple holding hands, an electric organ and a nest-egg representing $5,000. I put the wheel in a prominent place where I saw it constantly and just waited for the dreams to materialize", she laughed.

Within a few weeks she was able to buy a new car at a price she could afford. In December a traveling gospel quartet presented a program at her church and she was attracted to one of the singers. In February of 1971, the singer left the quartet, took a job in Dallas and married her.

In May her husband presented her with an organ for their home.

There was only one dream yet to be fulfilled. The $5,000 nest-egg. Now she has that and more. For all her dreams were realized within a year.

The beauty of this story is . . . we all have this capability, so let's discuss how one can accomplish this and how it works.

Do you know what you really want? Don't be too quick with your answer because the average person has so many wants, desires, wishes. They change daily with his moods. You are not able to give yourself the chance to generate enough energy for your end result if you vacillate.

THE NAME IT AND CLAIM IT GAME

We suggest you play a mental game with yourself. Ask yourself, "what is the most important goal I wish to accomplish?" Think about it seriously. Is it positive, constructive and creative? Sort of image the having it . . feel how it feels to have it. How will it change your life style.

A word of advice . . you need never involve another person to obtain your end result. Imposing your will on others is a NO NO and is really not necessary. Let me give you an example: You are working in an office position. Your boss is a fink . . he goofs off, there is only one way to do things, his way. You feel he lacks the knowledge for this position and you know you could do 100 percent better, plus you certainly would like the money that job offers. You want his job. You might entertain the idea he gets fired or the higher boss gets wise to him as you have, and at last you get the position you should have had all along. Granted we all fantasy this type situation at times. We dismiss it because our mind gets busy on other ideas.

What I'm saying is . . if you kept up this thought long and strong enough for it to become an obsession chances are that it would happen in due time. THIS IS NOT THE WAY TO PLAY THE GAME. You can obtain the same end results with peace of mind and not have to manipulate people and enjoy your achievements with this method. "I desire the perfect job with perfect pay;" that is all that is necessary. Every time your job comes to mind, repeat this phrase silently or think about it. With this as an end result it will work its way to fruition. In the course of time, your boss may be transferred, resign or whatever, or you may even be offered another job with another firm that may meet all your needs. There is no need to set things up . . just watch how it falls in place. For if this is truly your end result and you use proper mental desire, you will accomplish it.

One of the finest publications that goes into detail on a plan to accomplish a goal is titled IT WORKS by R.H.J., published by Scrivener and Co., and distributed by DeVorss & Co., 1641 Lincoln Blvd., Santa Monica, Calif. 90404.

As I lecture throughout the United States I get questions from the audiences in regard to particular situations. I also ask them if they wish to write and tell me their experiences of how they obtained their end result. The following is a recent incident that happened.

"But I don't enter contests and I don't feel that I can afford the money out of the family budget for my desire", said one of the women who was in the audience as I lectured to a group in a small Texas community. Her desire was to take a trip to the Bahamas. Seems like one of her friends had taken the leisure cruise and had related her experience and it so impressed the lady that she too wanted to make the voyage. Her husband, however, did not share her enthusiasm, but that did not dampen her desire.

I suggested she continue to project energy and know that her wish would come true.

Four weeks later is when I received the post card with a picture of a ship postmarked from the Bahamas. The card merely stated, "*It worked*" and her signature.

Upon her return home she wrote me the details how this all came about: While taking art classes she got acquainted with one of the other students in her class. The student, who was a distributor for women's cosmetics told the lady that the company she worked for was having a sales contest and the person in each district with the largest sales would win a trip to the Bahamas. She was confident she would win the trip as to date she had submitted the largest amount of sales. That is when the lady told her of her desire to take such a trip. She wished her artist friend success on her win and that her trip would be all she had hoped for.

A week later she received a phone call from the artist friend. She had won the trip, was ready to leave when her son suddenly became ill and had to undergo an appendectomy. She couldn't leave under these conditions, she knew of no one in her family that could make or want the trip on such short notice and if it was not taken it would be lost as it was a pre-planned package deal. So if she wanted the trip . . . it was hers free with no strings attached. Of course she accepted and was elated because the experience was everything she had hoped for. She confessed she was amazed how quickly everything fell into place.

Recently I met a woman in one of the shopping centers in Dallas who recognized me. She heard my lecture on WINeuvers for WISHcraft and immediately applied it. She had to share her success. She and her husband had just moved into a new home and were in the process of furnishing it. After hearing my lecture she knew what her desire would be. She wanted a china cabinet just like her grandmother had. She recalled how she admired the piece of furniture whenever she visited in her grandmother's home. When her grandmother passed away her estate was sold and distributed and no one seemed to know just where the china cabinet now was. Nevertheless this was her desire to have placed against one wall in her breakfast area the china cabinet or a duplicate.

Several weeks later her friend asked her to accompany her to an antique furniture store. She went and there was the china cabinet. If it had not been the original, the one owned by her former grandmother, it certainly was its twin. There was no difference. She was delighted until she heard the cost. "But that didn't deflate me and I didn't entertain any doubt that I would have it", she assured me.

"I told my husband about it and he went to look at it. He agreed it certainly would be perfect for the breakfast area but at this time our budget could not handle it. We left the store and on the way home my husband carefully explained the many reasons we could not afford it. I listened and said nothing. I can honestly tell you I did not mention the china cabinet again. I merely knew it was mine and visualized it standing against the bare wall.

"Two months later when a delivery truck backed into our driveway I thought they had the wrong house. The man that rang the doorbell asked me where I wanted the china cabinet placed. Shortly later, when my husband arrived home, he found me in tears as I was stroking the beautiful carvings on my polished china cabinet. He, too, knew it was mine and found no problem paying for it because the day he chose to go back and look at it again, in hopes he could get it at a reduced price, he found to his delight it had been marked down to half price as the store was in the process of moving to a new location and had reduced all their merchandise for quick removal."

Some of you might be saying "That's not so great . . . I always get what I'm after when I nag long enough". Another might think, "My, what an unusual husband she has . . . mine would be too tight". Still others may not even want an antique china cabinet.

The moral of these stories is . . . no naggin', no negative thinking that the price made it unobtainable . . . just steady positive energy and a knowing it would be her china cabinet.

I have to admire this beautiful positive attitude because she then told me she was working on another major goal that she knew would materialize soon.

What is your pleasure? Don't just sit there . . . get started.

— THE END OF MY BOOK —

THE BEGINNING
FOR A NEW WAY OF LIFE FOR YOU

ADDED EXPERIENCES

It has been almost three years since I first published my experiences. We are now on the 3rd printing of this book.

"So what have you won lately?" is one of the questions I'm asked quite frequently. For the last few years I have been doing more studying, living, experiencing and have traveled the country lecturing on subjects of positive thinking, ESP and powers of the mind. My thinking and beliefs have changed . . my how they've changed. The things that were once so important—I've come to realize the nothingness of them. The contesting game to win prizes is behind me. I achieved it. I enjoyed it and the need to prove something to myself and others is gone.

To replace it came the realization that life is a game, planet earth is but a classroom of learning. We are here to overcome, understand and experience. We outgrow needs, desires, places and things. This is not new to some of you I am sure.

The most significant experience I've accomplished to date is my awareness as a lecturer. From the correspondence I receive and comments expressed by persons . . they claim to have benefited from the information I've shared. However, I *know* I have learned the most.

I realize people are on all levels of awareness. I respect their concepts, listen with concern and know that it truly is very much of a do-it-yourself world. Yes we need people . . but they cannot do or experience for us. We as individuals are powerful, we are what we think. It's high time we all reach this point of knowing. For if we do not like our station in life, our job, our selves we can change it. It must begin first by changing our thinking. It must also be a sincere desire . . then things start happening. That's not new either is it? I agree with you. It is not new, but there is one difference. Awareness and knowing are different . . as saying and doing.

Life is such a beautiful experience when you learn to live instead of just exist . . learn to feel instead of just touch . . learn to truly observe instead of just look . . learn to listen instead of just hear. And most important learn to say something instead of just talk.

There is a saying that is expressed thus: "Physically we are what we eat. Mentally we are what we think. Spiritually we are what we believe." Precedence should be placed on the last statement. We are what we believe.

One of the most successful methods of achieving this is by making a P tape (Personalized tape for your particular need system). Listen to it on a daily basis until you believe it. You can actually change your mental and physical body up to a point. Some schools of thought call it Mind over Matter, whatever frame of reference you choose to express, it is successful. Does everyone have this ability? I would say yes. However not everyone has the faith that is theirs and will work for them.

To cultivate faith in yourself is to KNOW. Some

might confuse being so positive with bullheadedness or being dogmatic. There is a difference. Let me share a concept of faith with you.

Faith is a KNOWING that what you ask for is already granted. You KNOW it. A feeling of calmness, confidence takes over. No person on earth could change your mind or sway you. Nothing remains but the manifestation of it. Many times that takes place almost immediately. I will again repeat from an earlier chapter. There are no failures . . only a delay in results. So as one of our colorful personalities states, "KEEP THE FAITH".

There is so much to see . . . to do . . to experience and to write about that I will shortly be publishing a second book. Also I will continue to lecture on a limited basis, to counsel persons who need to realize they have their answers, and above all to practice what I preach.

Sincerely,

Helen Hadsell